GERMAN YOUTH, YOUR LEADER!

BOOKS FROM CLEMENS & BLAIR
— www.clemensandblair.com —

For My Legionnaires, by Corneliu Codreanu
Myth and Sun, by Martin Friedrich
Unmasking Anne Frank, by Ikuo Suzuki
Pan-Judah! Political Cartoons of Der Stürmer, by Robert Penman
Passovers of Blood, by Ariel Toaff
The Poisonous Mushroom, by Ernst Hiemer
On the Jews and Their Lies, by Martin Luther
Mein Kampf, by Adolf Hitler
Mein Kampf (Dual English-German edition), by Adolf Hitler
The Essential Mein Kampf, by Adolf Hitler
The Myth of the 20th Century, by Alfred Rosenberg

BOOKS BY THOMAS DALTON
— www.thomasdaltonphd.com —

The Steep Climb: Essays on the Jewish Question
Classic Essays on the Jewish Question: 1850 to 1945
Debating the Holocaust
The Holocaust: An Introduction
The Jewish Hand in the World Wars
Eternal Strangers: Critical Views of Jews and Judaism
Hitler on the Jews
Goebbels on the Jews
Streicher, Rosenberg, and the Jews: The Nuremberg Transcripts

GERMAN YOUTH, YOUR LEADER!

Edited by
Thomas Dalton, PhD

Drawings by
Philipp ('Fips') Rupprecht

Colorization by
Robert Penman

Clemens & Blair, LLC
— 2023 —

CLEMENS & BLAIR, LLC

Copyright © 2023, by Thomas Dalton, editor

All rights reserved. No part of this publication may be reproduced, stored in a retrieval system, or transmitted, in any form or by any means, electronic, mechanical, photocopying, recording, or otherwise.

Clemens & Blair, LLC, is a non-profit educational publisher.
www.clemensandblair.com

Library of Congress Cataloging-in-Publication Data

Dalton, Thomas (ed.)
German Youth, Your Leader!

p. cm.
Includes bibliographical references

ISBN 979-8986-7250-79
(pbk.: alk. paper)

1. National Socialism
2. Germany, history of (20th century)

Printing number: 9 8 7 6 5 4 3 2 1

Printed in the United States of America on acid-free paper.

DEDICATION

This book is dedicated to all the young men and women of the world who will have to grapple with the Jewish Question at some point in their lives—the sooner, the better.

CONTENTS

INTRODUCTION by Thomas Dalton   i

Chapter 1: Hitler's Youth   **1**
    His Parents' Home   1
    History was his Favorite Subject   6
    The Young Revolutionary   8
    Alone in the World, Without Father or Mother   12
    The Day Laborer   16

Chapter 2: Munich, his Second Home   **23**
    The War Volunteer   23
    For Conspicuous Valor   29
    The War-Blinded   31
    The Politician   33
    November 9, 1923   37
    Hitler in Landsberg   37

Chapter 3: The Struggle for Power   **39**
    The Organizer   39
    Further Attempts at Suppression   41
    Towards the Goal   45
    The Speaker   46
    The Imperial Chancellor   50
    The Day of Potsdam   52

FURTHER READING   57

APPENDIX   59

ACKNOWLEDGMENT

The editor would like to acknowledge the assistance of Ms. Mildred Grau in the translation of this text from the German original.

The editor also recognizes the outstanding artistic work of restoration and coloration of all the following Fips images by Robert Penman. His work is truly exceptional; it brings an intensity to this book that would otherwise be lacking. These colorized Fips drawings make Hitler's life-story shine like never before.

GERMAN YOUTH, YOUR LEADER!

INTRODUCTION
THOMAS DALTON

For many years now, academia, Hollywood, and the mainstream media have horribly misrepresented the events of World War Two. We all know the standard account: an evil man, Adolf Hitler, climbed to power in 1930s Germany by a combination of demagoguery, lies, and manipulation. He was a fanatical Jew-hater and used the Jews as scapegoats for all of Germany's problems. He was also intent on world domination and so, in 1939, he started a World War. Thanks only to the bravery of the Allies—especially the British and the Americans—the world was saved from the evil Nazis, and Hitler was destroyed. Sadly, during the war, Hitler managed to kill 6 million Jews, most of them in gas chambers. This "Holocaust" was one of greatest crimes in human history.

The problem with this, of course, is that *nearly all of it is wrong*—much of it, intentionally so. Let me start by laying out a truthful picture of the man, his life, and World War Two. Adolf Hitler in fact had a normal and happy childhood, and he demonstrated early on certain special qualities of focus, intensity, determination, and leadership. As a young man, his desire was to be an artist and an architect, and he conducted his schooling around this goal. Unfortunately, his father died when he was 13, and then his mother when he was 15. Making his way on his own, he traveled to Vienna to develop his training in art and architecture. Working as a manual laborer to earn a meager living, he got a tough education in 'the school of life.' It was there also that got interested in politics and especially in the Jewish Question: how society should respond to a malicious and self-interested Jewish minority in its midst.

Giving up on Vienna after several years, he moved to Munich in 1912, when he was 23 years old—a city he found much more to his liking, given its thoroughly German character. There he developed his central philosophical outlook: that the Germanic people should join together to create a single, unified nation, and should oppose the growing threat of Russian communism and Marxism ("the Reds"). In June of 1914, Archduke Ferdinand was shot, and within two months, World War One had begun. Hitler enlisted in the German army, fighting bravely on the front line for over four years. He was injured, recovered, returned to the front, and then injured again for a second time, in October 1918. While recovering from his second injury, a "revolution" occurred in Germany, driven in large part by Jews and Marxists who wanted to overthrow the German leader, Kaiser Wilhelm II—which they did.

With the Kaiser gone, Jewish Marxists took charge of Germany and surrendered to England and France, and then proceeded to establish their own form of government known as the Weimar Republic. For Hitler, the surrender was a "stab in the back" of the German people, so that a group of militant Jews could take power; this naturally deepened his resentment of them.

Hitler became politically active, eventually forming a new political party: the National Socialist German Workers' Party, or NSDAP. Their enemies called them 'Nazis' for short. With Hitler in the lead, the party grew rapidly, and by 1920 it became a potent force in Bavaria and southern Germany.

In November 1923, Hitler and others attempted an overthrow of the corrupt local government in Munich, but they failed; he was imprisoned for almost a year. Once freed, he built up the NSDAP into a nationwide party and continued to gain support in elections throughout the 1920s and early 1930s. By January of 1933, Hitler was named Chancellor of Germany.

As leader of his nation, Hitler immediately began to right the wrongs of the Jewish Weimar regime, and the German people prospered—even as the rest of the industrial world was mired in a global depression. Hitler recovered the economy, built up heavy industry, eliminated unemployment, and strengthened the military. As a part of this process, he managed to remove Jews from their positions of dominance, encouraging many to leave the country. In March 1938, and with the support of the Austrian people, Germany annexed Austria into the newly-expanded German Reich. Again, this was consistent with Hitler's goal of unifying all Germanic people under a single national government.

In September 1939, Hitler sought to retake territory in Poland that had been seized from Germany after World War One; this would also protect the rights of the many German people who were living there. His army crossed into Poland, quickly retaking the land. Within two days, England and France—which had treaties with Poland against "German aggression"—declared war on Germany. At the same time, and in agreement with Germany, Russia invaded Poland from the Eastern side. Thus, very quickly, much of Europe was technically at war.

The story of this war is long and complex, and I won't try to cover the details here. In short, Hitler realized that Soviet Russia, run primarily by Jewish Marxists, posed a mortal threat to Germany and all of Europe. At the same time, Jewish capitalists in England, France, and the US actively sought to destroy Hitler simply because he wanted a 'Germany for the Germans' and believed that Jews should not be running his country. Thus, American Jews prodded and pushed president Roosevelt (himself part-Jewish) to support England and France and eventually, after the Pearl Harbor attack by Japan, to declare war on Germany.

As a result, Hitler was effectively fighting two wars at once: against the Soviet Union to his east, and against England, France, and the US to his west. Even for the well-trained and disciplined German military, it was an impossible situation; enemy forces eventually closed in on both sides, bombing cities and killing thousands of German civilians—women, children, and the elderly—along the way. In the end, Germany was forced to surrender; Hitler and his second-in-command, Joseph Goebbels, committed suicide to avoid capture.

What about the "Holocaust"? During the war, as Jews were increasingly confined to labor camps or transferred to captured territory in the East, many naturally died along the way—after all, conditions were difficult for everyone in Germany at that time. Some famous camps, like Auschwitz and Majdanek, were primarily work camps where Jews were forced to support the war effort. Other camps, like Treblinka and Belzec, were transfer facilities where Jews were held for a time, disinfected from typhus and other diseases, and then shipped on further east, where many were abandoned.

Amidst this whole process, involving hundreds of thousands of Jews, many died from disease, injury, illness, or suicide. Many were shot, especially if they fought back or collaborated with the enemy. However, there was never any "systematic extermination plan" by Hitler in which gas chambers were used to kill masses of Jews. There were "gas chambers," but they were all rooms used to disinfect clothing, linen, and personal items from disease-carrying lice. None were used to kill people, despite what many people want us to think today. In the end, about 500,000 Jews perished, from all causes, during the war. This is a tragic figure, but it is far less than the 6 million that is often claimed today.

In sum: Hitler was a courageous and visionary leader, someone who only wanted the best for his German people. In his desire to free his nation from Jews—both internal and external—he became a target of global Jewry, who used all their might to attack and destroy him. As a result, around 60 million people died overall in the war. And even today, 80 years later, in the "victorious" nations, a powerful Jewish Lobby continues to dominate politics, economics, education, and the media. They continue to demonize and attack anyone who might want to live free from Jewish influence. They continue to censor free speech and to distort history, so that no one—especially no young people—will know the truth.

About This Book: *German Youth, Your Leader!*

Sometime in 1933 or 1934, the German leadership—then under Hitler—decided that they needed to write a proper history of Hitler's life, especially for German school-aged children between the ages of about 10 and 17. Thus, the government decided to write short textbooks for their students. Today, we know about two of these: *Deutsche Jugend, Dein Führer!* ("German Youth, Your Leader!") and a slightly longer work, *Aufbruch der Nation* ("Dawn of the Nation"). The books would have both text and pictures; the pictures would be drawn by a famous German artist, Philipp ("Fips") Rupprecht. Fips was most well-known for his cartoons and other drawings in the newspaper *Der Stürmer*, but he also drew images for other books as well.

The original Fips images were all done in black-and-white, since color printing was expensive and very rare back in the 1930s. Figure 1 shows a typical image as it appeared in the original German text. Now, in this new edition, all the images have been fully restored and colorized by a talented digital artist, Robert Penman. Figure 2 shows the same image in colorized form; clearly it has much more impact now. We can believe that Fips would be very happy to see the quality of our restorations here. (The Appendix includes some photographs of the original German book, including Fips images.)

Figure 1. Original Fips drawing. Figure 2. Colorization by R. Penman.

The present book, aimed at youth between 10 and 15 years of age, was almost lost to history. Very few copies survived the war, and almost no one in the victorious nations wanted to talk about them. Fortunately, we have been able to recover both books and to translate them into English, for present-day youth, teens, and others interested in the Hitler era.

We know only a few other details about these books. They were published under the direction of Hans Schemm, the Director of the Bavarian Ministry of Education and the head of the National Socialist Teachers' Union. The books were written and edited by "leading persons in the Teachers' Union," although we have no specific names. We do not know exactly when they were published, although we can presume it was 1934 or perhaps even late 1933 (Schemm was tragically killed in an airplane crash in March 1935, at the age of 43). Other than these few details, we have only the text itself, which is clear, accurate, and highly relevant for young people wanting to know about the life history of this man, Adolf Hitler.

Today, some 90 years after their initial publication, we see these books in a new light. They have a deep relevance for all—youth, teens, young adults, and others. But we need to keep a few things in mind as we read this book. First, the text was obviously written while Hitler was still alive and expected to rule for many years. He was around 45 years old, a very young leader by today's standards. His energy and vision were only beginning to reveal themselves. The future was bright for the German nation, and the youth were expected to play an important role.

Second, the writers of this book had, of course, no idea of a looming World War. They could not anticipate the coming tragedy, nor the boundless depths of Jewish hatred that would move nations against Germany simply because she wished to be free, independent, and self-governing.

Third, this is a direct, unaltered, and uncorrupted view of the National Socialist perspective, something that is almost impossible to find today. It is no exaggeration to say that every modern text on Hitler or the war is slanted, tendentious, hostile, deceptive, or malicious. Most are written or published by Jews. It is virtually impossible for the average person, or the average student, to get a true, accurate, and honest account. Of course, this text, being sympathetic to Hitler, will tend to emphasize the positives of his life and downplay any negatives. But this alone is helpful because it serves as a counterbalance to the horribly slanted conventional story. Furthermore, it is a totally accurate view of what the Germans were saying to their own youth—it is their very textbook, after all. Here, we get to hear from prominent National Socialists *in their own words*, direct and unedited. Here, we get to read passages directly from Hitler's own book, *Mein Kampf*—in his own words. Such things never happen today. It may be hard to believe, but there are many scholars, professors, historians, and other "experts" who have never read *Mein Kampf* and know nothing of what Hitler actually wrote. It seems almost ridiculous, but a teen reader of this book will likely know more of *Mein Kampf* than nearly every college professor, and he will certainly know more about Hitler's life; such is the sad state of affairs in the modern world. This is what happens when a powerful Jewish Lobby controls what we read and think.

Fourth, this small book is, of course, only a start to learning about Hitler and National Socialism. The reader is invited to review the short "Further Reading" section at the end of this book to find other sources of reliable and unbiased information.

Lastly, the title: It was obviously addressed to the German youth of the day, to help them gain knowledge and respect for their leader, the Führer, who was alive and well at the time. I have elected to retain the original title, even though we may now consider this book directed at all youth, the youth of the world—all those who might wish to know about a great leader of the past century, and a man whose ideas can yet serve as inspiration and a guiding light. In a sense, this book could now be titled *Youth of the World, Your Guiding Light!* Hitler is still, even today, a true guide—*ein Führer*—for those who seek the truth.

People everywhere, young and old, have much to learn from the true story of Adolf Hitler—a story that is virtually never heard today. The "powers that be" continue to make every effort to confuse, censor, and misinform the public, and to implicitly and explicitly slander anything to do with Hitler or National Socialism. They well know the power of that man and his ideas.

And this is precisely why you, the reader, need to know them too.

— Thomas Dalton, PhD

GERMAN YOUTH, YOUR LEADER!

Chapter 1
Hitler's Youth

His Parents' Home

More than 100 years ago, the bookseller Johann Philipp Palm was captured by the French for distributing a pamphlet titled "Germany in its Deepest Humiliation." He was taken to the French fortress of Braunau, where he was shot four days later. No one suspected at that time that this site, soaked with the martyr's blood of a German hero, would one day be the birthplace of the greatest statesman of our age, Adolf Hitler. From this blood came the avenger of the German people.

Braunau is located directly on the Bavarian-Austrian border, which is formed by the Inn River. Adolf Hitler was born there, the son of customs officer Alois Hitler and his wife Klara. Not long after his birth, his father was transferred to Passau. In order to provide his family with a longstanding home, he bought a rural property in the nearby village of Hafeld, which was the family's home for a long period of time. He himself could only return there on Sundays, as his strenuous employment did not allow it. Later Alois took leave and became a farmer again, as his fathers had once been.

These were happy years, in which the young boy Adolf was allowed to spend in his parents' country house, in a landscape blessed with grain fields, meadows, and gardens. Everything a boy's heart could desire was offered to him—to climb the birch and alder trees towering to the sky, to jump in the brook that flowed close to his father's garden. The boy also enjoyed working on the farm. He had a special affection for the farm's young animals, with whom he frolicked and played as if they were his best companions. His favorite playmates were his dogs, whose loyal devotion he still holds in high esteem today.

Unfortunately, the school conditions there were so poor that the father, for the sake of the children's education, was forced to sell the property he had grown so fond of and move to Lambach. Here the young Adolf dreamed of the first ideals of his life. The reputation and reverence of the local parson awakened in him the desire to one day become a pastor or abbot of a monastery. His effervescent, lively nature was noticed by all and won him the admiration and love of his schoolmates. The ecclesiastic festivals of the local Canons held a great attraction for him. It was not uncommon for him to take part in the chorus at festivals, which fascinated and captivated him so much that he was completely intoxicated by their grandeur and pageantry. Nevertheless, he was not a meek boy or a coward; he even committed the great crime of smoking as a schoolboy. (He does not smoke at all today.)

Concern about the children's future prompted father Alois once again to take up the walking stick to provide them with a better education. His greatest wish was that Adolf would become a higher civil servant. Therefore, he sought to have Adolf attend a secondary school, and chose a *Realschule* for him. The one was in Linz. But in order to reduce expenses, Alois preferred to move to the nearby village of Leonding, where the family took up residence in a small house right next to the cemetery wall. The long road to school gave young Adolf occasion and opportunity for the boldest undertakings and youthful escapades—but these never got out of hand. Even then, he demanded complete respect and discipline from his playmates, and he refused to be the leader of a loose pack of scoundrels. Many times, he gave speeches to his classmates, which often ended in a duel of words, from which he always emerged victorious. It was clear that, even then, he had the desire to become a great orator.

At school, Hitler soon won the goodwill of the teachers as well as the respect of his classmates. He learned very easily and with deep understanding. His favorite subjects were history and drawing, but he also excelled in the others. When his father, however, insisted more and more that he should choose the career path of a civil servant, his son had to answer him with a firm "no." It pained him greatly to have to disappoint his dear father in this regard and to declare his opposition based on his strong inclination to a free profession. He loved freedom more than anything else.

In addition, his dream was to become a painter. When Hitler expressed this wish to his father, Alois was horrified and shouted at him: "As long as I live, never — never! I cannot give in; otherwise, you might go hungry, and this would ruin all my efforts and troubles to help you out." Hitler was silent. He knew that he had to avoid further arguments with his father about his future. He was even more defiant at school, and believed that he might get his way if he neglected his studies. Thus, it happened that the next evaluation of his school work was particularly bad. In history, geography, and drawing, he was excellent, while the other subjects were graded merely "adequate," if not "unsatisfactory."

History was his Favorite Subject

"From now on, I raved about everything that had anything to do with war or soldiering."

Those who know history, know and love their people. Even as a boy, Hitler was deeply interested in his favorite subjects: geography and history. He was also fortunate to have an extraordinarily talented teacher in this subject, someone who knew how to introduce his pupils to the deeper context of the life of nations. The Führer still recalls, with the greatest of reverence, this history teacher: Professor Dr. Leopold Pötsch, at the secondary school in Linz. In the words of Hitler himself, he understood not only how "to illuminate the past from the present, but also how to draw the consequences for the present from the past."

So, history lessons became, for young Adolf, hours of inner enlightenment and joy. What German boy would not have felt the same inner fire and enthusiasm, with a teacher who really understood how to portray the great deeds of our ancestors in a warm and emotional way? In particular, it was the glorious achievements of the German armies in the 1870s that captivated the boy.

As a special stroke of luck, he came across an edition of a book called *The Franco-Prussian War of 1870/71* while browsing his father's library. The two volumes were richly illustrated, and from then on, they became the boy's secret pleasure. He could think of nothing better than withdrawing to some quiet corner with his favorite book and envisioning the great events of our fathers in words and pictures. This awakened in young Adolf a passionate love of soldiering and heroism.

The boy's inquiring mind, however, very soon came to insights that were later to become the foundations of the great statesman's teachings.

Regarding this, the Führer himself said:

"This would become important to me in other respects as well. For the first time, the question was pressed upon me, however vaguely I imagined it: Whether, and what difference there was, between the Germans fighting these battles and the Austrians? Why hadn't Austria also fought in this war? Why hadn't my father and all the others fought, too? Aren't we Austrians the same as all other Germans? Don't we all belong together? This problem started burrowing into my mind for the first time."

Even then, the boy developed the worldview that he later would be able to imprint upon his generation: a doctrine of the unchangeable foundations of a people, *of blood and soil* as the only prerequisites for the life of the people. The young Hitler not only had love for the people in his heart, but also the knowledge in his mind that all Germans belong together according to blood and race, and not separated by any national borders. Thus, we already see in the youthful Hitler the worldview of our time. Like all the truly great men of our people, such as Bismarck and Martin Luther, Hitler confirms the insight that even the early years of youth show the clear outlines of the tremendous creativity and the character of a great statesman.

The Young Revolutionary

*"I was anything but a good boy in the common sense.
I became a little ringleader."*

The Führer tells us that he learned easily and very well in school, "but was otherwise rather difficult to deal with." His superb powers of comprehension, and his rich inner life—which is particularly characterized by sudden, lightning-like inspirations—enabled him to manage quickly and thoroughly with the class material. His clear mind quickly recognized the need to distinguish the essential from the non-essential, and thus acquired a deeply-rooted, coherent body of knowledge.

The gifted student then had enough time to devote himself not only to household chores, but also to cavorting in the open air with his friends. His parents' home offered him ample opportunity for this. Hitler had the good fortune to spend his youth in the countryside, in fields, meadows, and forests. The boy's courage and determination, the spirit of enterprise, and joy in action developed rapidly. Even as a boy, it was in his singular nature to overcome existing difficulties and to gladly and gallantly take up the fight with his peers at any time. Bumps and wounds were willingly accepted. But he couldn't bear the thought of not being able to achieve anything in life. If he had suffered pain or a wound in an argument with his often-robust young friends, he hated, for example, to seek help from his caring mother. The boy's independence and courageous enduring of the discomforts of life were already inherent in his earliest youth.

There was nothing he despised so much as being effeminate, being a homebody. Just as the character of an adult can only be formed "in the current of the world," so in the case of children, only contact with peers can form the basis for later struggles in life.

He therefore learned very early on to deal with the dark side of people. He knew how to bear with silence the naughtiness of his comrades, and the mistakes made that would certainly have resulted in punishment. To be sure, he appealed to the conscience of his young friends. With all urgency, he knew how to tackle injustice. But if someone repeated the crimes, and warnings and friendly rebukes didn't help, he could also be firm and renounce a friendship for a while, or even forever.

The gifted boy, whose strong character quickly made itself known to his friends, was, of course, not lacking in hostilities from some of his contemporaries. Young Adolf often stood alone in disputes, and yet found the spirit and the knowledge to grapple with a useless crowd.

One of Hitler's classmates wrote about such an event: One day after school, a gang of boys yelled out, "Let's scrub that Hitler." On to the fight! Hitler, of course, had no inkling of the planned attack. Now, realizing what was about to happen, he didn't run away like others would have done in such a case, but accepted the fight, even though he had little chance of success. But the "scrubbing" wasn't as easy as the gang had thought. Hitler fought back bravely; it was an eye for an eye, a tooth for a tooth. In order to have freedom of movement and not get tangled up, he broke away from the crowd and pulled back, step by step, always looking for cover. If one of the attackers got close, he was immediately punched down. He continued this type of combat until his opponents gave up the fight. The tough gang came to know and respect their opponent.

The next few days already brought friendly approaches and all kinds of offers of alliances. Despite all the fighting with his peers, it never occurred to him to appeal to his teacher or his parents for protection. That would have been too embarrassing. He saw a great virtue in the capacity to bear injustice without immediately crying out for punishment. He hated the lack of reserve of his jabbering schoolmates, and considered it particularly unworthy of a German boy, to tattle or blabber—either out of maliciousness or even in order to gain an advantage. Such a boy seemed to lack character, and could even later become dangerous for the people and the Fatherland.

Soon, young Hitler's leadership qualities became evident. He often had an educational effect on his friends, with an inspiring speech. Very soon, they recognized his clear superiority. Often he succeeded in provoking even the quiet and reserved boys to the most audacious pranks with a fiery rant. It often got quite rambunctious in the process; to the horror of his parents and especially his good mother, bitter complaints came in about the "ringleader" who incited the others. Of course, perceptive people also recognized the genius of the youngster, who not only attracted attention with his excellent performance in school, but also showed very clear leadership qualities when playing on the street or in the field. In war games, the side with Adolf Hitler as its leader always won.

Thus, before long, the boy's character was strengthened in the battles. He needed his comrades, with all their virtues and vices. He commanded them. They followed him. They provided him with resistance, and they put obstacles in his way, all of which could only help him develop his own will and strengthen his resolve. He who wants to become a master must cultivates this, in due time. The foundation for his later life as Führer was already laid at that time in Lambach and Leonding.

Alone in the World, Without a Father or Mother

Unfortunately, the carefree, happy life of the young boy was all too soon overshadowed by dark portents and gloom.

His father died suddenly. A terrible loss for the son, to no longer have his father at his side—a father who was gifted with a strong will and great determination!

His mother clung to the father's wishes, and after his death, she did not accept her son's desire. She too thought that she could not bear the responsibility of consenting that he become an artist (a painter). Hitler complied with the wishes of his beloved mother; he was determined to complete the *Realschule*, since the knowledge gained would certainly be useful in later life. But then he was stricken with a lung disease that kept him from attending school for a long period of time. On the advice of his doctor, he suspended his studies for a full year, even after his recovery. The doctor advised the worried mother to take the boy's physical condition into account when choosing a profession. In any case, the doctor considered office work inappropriate for the boy's weakened body. Hitler considered it an intervention of fate, and was glad to finally see his dearest wish come true.

Regrettably, providence would have it otherwise. A terrible stroke of fate hit the young man: his mother, who had been in poor health for a long time, died. Hitler said that this blow struck him particularly horribly. "I had idolized my father, but I loved my mother."

Now the boy stood alone as an orphan, completely abandoned in a bleak, cold, and heartless world. Fate forced him to shape his own life and confronted him already with hard decisions, even in his youngest years. "Poverty and harsh reality now forced me to make a quick resolution. My father's limited finances had been largely exhausted by my mother's serious illness; my orphan's pension was not enough even to be able to live on, so I now had to depend on myself to somehow earn my bread."

1 — Hitler's Youth

The boy's parting from his parents' grave was bitter. "Twice in my life I have cried," Hitler said, "once, at the grave of his mother, and then in November 1918, given the shame of the Fatherland, when it collapsed." For him, the memory of his mother, that fine and tender woman who sacrificed herself for her son with her feeble strength, was eternal and imperishable.

With a clear conscience, he preserved the memory of his parents. He was the faithful, obedient, and honest son of his parents, without guilt and without remorse, accompanied by the undying love of his mother and guarded by a merciful God.

This was how the young Hitler started his way in life. The highest purpose of life for him was to one day be able to stand before his own parents, before the people, and before the Lord God, with his soul and conscience intact. "May my conscience always be awake and warn me when it is necessary, so that no one deceives me and I do not disappoint others." The path from his parents' grave to the Garrison Church of Potsdam—where Hitler was granted power by Von Hindenburg in 1933—was a long one, filled with heated battles and accompanied by extraordinary achievements and world-historical victories. But at the beginning and at the end, as well as in the middle, there is the old German folk saying: "Always be faithful and honest until the day you die, and do not deviate a hair's breadth from the ways of God."

The next target for Hitler was now the cosmopolitan city of Vienna, which had once already attracted his father and would become a decisive factor in his life. "With a suitcase of clothes and linen in my hands, and with an unshakable will in my heart, I went to Vienna. What my father had accomplished 50 years earlier, I, too, hoped to snatch away from fate."

He seized it, and even a bit more!

Arrival in Vienna

The Day Laborer

"Five years of misery and suffering for me in this Phaeacian city."
— *Hitler*

Still half a boy, with his few belongings, linen, and clothes packed together in a suitcase, Hitler got off the train in Vienna. He had only 50 guilders in cash, which he wanted to keep as a nest egg. But he also wanted to eat, and he had to have a roof over his head. That costs money and more money.

As a result, he had to look for work, which was not so easy to find in Vienna at that time. The large army of senior officers, civil servants, artists, and scholars, and the large influx of the most-respected men from all countries, made the city appear as a metropolis of splendor in Europe. The glittering parties in the palaces of the Ringstrasse, which lasted until the early morning hours, were known all over the world. Because of them and because of the many other places of entertainment that Vienna had to offer, it became a center of attraction for high society, near and far—a light-hearted, international, cosmopolitan city. To this day, one finds in Vienna representatives of all nations that have secretly made their home in the so-called "City of Songs." If Vienna had, in this regard, an undisputed world reputation, it was also inevitable that it had an unstoppable stream of people from the countryside, all looking for work, who wanted to find their fortune in the capital. At that time, no other city in Europe had as many unemployed and homeless people as Vienna. Thousands had no bread, and just as many had no home. They were forced to spend their nights on park benches or under the arches of a bridge. And then every morning, they all began to hunt for work. Nothing was overlooked.

Hitler, too, had no other choice. He applied for work on some construction sites—but in vain. Next, he tried to find work as a draftsman, because he wanted to become a master builder and remain in the construction trade.

As a construction worker

However, since he had neither attended a school of construction nor passed a journeyman's examination, he was always turned away. One contractor took Hitler's plea to heart, because he said to him: "If you want to stay as a laborer, I will keep you." Hitler did not exactly want to, but he had to. Now he became a day laborer, a transient worker, for starvation wages.

He immediately had work assigned to him and was happy to have found a new life. There was little dignity with this profession, and indeed it was a heavy burden. It was not easy for the young man to wield a shovel from morning to night in the hot sun, or to carry heavy bricks to the top of the scaffolding. But even more difficult was handling his coworkers, who, because of his clean clothes, civilized speech, and reserved manner, saw Hitler as an oddball; they tried to shake him off with biting ridicule and contempt. Suddenly he had people around him whom he did not know and who had, initially, disgusted him because of their crudeness and wanton behavior.

Nevertheless, he tried to empathize with his fellow workers' way of thinking. It seemed unfair to him, to judge people only by their actions without taking the trouble to get to know their motivations. Soon it became clear to him that, with many of them, their brutal demeanor was often only an outward appearance; otherwise, they were governed by a fine and compassionate soul. Certainly, it did not remain hidden from him that, in a large number of his fellow workers, a compassion and sensitivity for others had been completely lost. The harsh battle for a bit of daily bread, the painful struggle for a position in life, had completely deadened their feelings for the misery and the general awareness for the plight of their fellow human beings. In this daily struggle with oneself, egoism—or only "thinking about oneself"—became the source of partisan disunity.

Hitler, who, until then, had heard little or nothing about it, would join this workers' organization. But he wasn't the kind of man to jump right in. It was important to him to get to know the idea of the organization first. From their speeches, he heard many things that he, too, agreed with. For example, they wanted to undermine the anti-German Habsburg state and bring it down. Hitler, too, was often angry when he saw how this Austrian state could only sustain itself through the millions of Germans living there, but it did next to nothing for their interests. For this reason, he had no love for this state either.

Then the workers wanted to fight for a better and more humane life for the poor, as he always heard. This also pleased him, and he long wished to join forces with such fighters.

However, when he read their newspapers and saw how they flirted with groups hostile to the German people, also asked these groups for help in their endeavors, or made promises to them, then this lack of character on the part of the German Social Democrat party disgusted him greatly. Thus, he no longer wanted to participate.

At this point, he began to diligently study the idea of Marxism, because he wanted to know whether it promoted love of the Fatherland, of the national community, and a military spirit. However, he found no such goals in their books, but rather he found the opposite: the communist song *"The Internationale,"* class struggle, and abolition of compulsory military service. When he understood this, he refused to join this criminal organization; he did not want to support such things that would cause the German people, whom he loved, to eventually perish.

Now he was hated, insulted, and persecuted. It came to such a point that, one day, Hitler gave up his job. If he had not left, they would have thrown him down from the scaffolding. Now he had to look for work elsewhere, but even there, he was no better off. So he wandered from one construction site to the next, and never tired of starting all over again, even though he knew that it wouldn't be long before he would again be out of a job.

Despite this, Hitler did not hate or despise his fellow workers. He knew too well that they were only mislead and therefore did not know what they were doing. The more they rejected him, the more he loved them. That is why he always thought about how to help these misguided people. It was incomprehensible to him that they were continually speaking against the nation, the Fatherland, and religion, as well as denigrating the schools, law, and morality. It became clear to him that, within Social Democracy, such incorrigible malice and reckless agitation against all the good institutions of the people and against the people themselves, could only come from a foreign element.

Through many years of studying the socialist press, he recognized the Jew as the spiritual originator of the vulgarity and discord that, little by little, disintegrated the people. At first, for reasons of personal restraint, he hesitated to say anything unfavorable about the Jews. But after spending a long time observing their appearances in public, in the press, art, literature, and in the theater, where they were always "front and center," and discovering everywhere the moral stains of "the chosen people," his thinking triumphed over feeling. And now, without hesitation, he included the Jewish Question in his discussions. He saw them as the ice-cold, enterprising conductors of the dens of vice in the big cities, and he recognized them as the leaders of Social Democracy. With this insight, he gained a true perspective; his long inner spiritual struggle over this question finally ended. Hitler now began to place the Jews at the center of his political thinking—as the fundamental evil.

In any case, he tirelessly continued his searched for higher knowledge. Theater, books, concerts, and even visits to Parliament provided him with ample stimulation. It is astonishing how he was able to improve his education and his knowledge with such limited financial means, and on top of his working hours. While other spent their free time in bars and cinemas, he used it to prepare himself for the difficult task in the future.

Finally, after much starving, working and studying, he left Vienna and moved to Munich; he had finished his studies at the University of

1 — Hitler's Youth 21

Life, which he experienced as a manual laborer. A few years later, the apprentice became the master builder of the German people.

Chapter 2
Munich, his Second Home

Five years of misery and suffering, the most desolate time of his life, lay behind Hitler when he left Vienna in the spring of 1912 and moved to Munich. But his time in Vienna had made him tough; it threw the reluctant young man into the world of suffering and poverty, and thus allowed him to get to know those people for whom he was later to fight.

In his book *Mein Kampf*, Hitler wrote about Munich:

> "Almost from the very first moment of my sojourn there, I came to love that city more than any other place I had known. A German city! How different from Vienna! It was with a feeling of disgust that I recalled that Babylon of races. … Today I am more attached to this city than any other; it will remain inseparably connected to the development of my own life. My feelings of inner happiness and satisfaction with the place can be attributed to the charm of the Residence of the Wittelsbachs; it has attracted probably everyone who is blessed with a feeling for beauty, as well as a calculating mind."

And even if he still struggled for his daily bread, a brighter, happier life began for him. Hitler had found a new home in Munich.

The War Volunteer

It came in July and August of the year 1914. Days of tremendous events occurred. The Austrian heir to the throne and his wife were murdered, war was declared on Serbia, and the mobilization of the German army was ordered. Germany transformed itself into a gray army camp. The World War had broken out and all of Europe was in flames. Hitler was deeply moved by the heroic courage of the German people in those memorable days of August.

2 — Munich

He tells it himself:

> "For me, these hours came as a deliverance from the distress that had weighed upon me during the days of my youth. I'm not ashamed to admit today that I was carried away by the enthusiasm of the moment. I sank down on my knees and thanked heaven, out of the fullness of my heart, for the good fortune of living at such a time."

Hundreds of thousands of German men and youths volunteered for war service. Hitler held Austrian citizenship. But he was not inclined to join the Austrian army, because he hated that unfortunate confederation of states. He wanted to serve in the *German* army. In short order, he petitioned the Bavarian king to join a Bavarian regiment. And that which he never thought possible quickly became a reality. The very next day, the postman brought the letter that fulfilled his fervent wish. Hardly had the postman left the room, when he fell to his knees to thank the Creator.

The Messenger

In the heaviest shell fire

2 — Munich

The very next day he was standing in the barracks yard, and soon wearing his field-gray soldier's uniform. The training period was hard, but he endured it with joy. Military trains rolled incessantly to both fronts. One fortress after another fell, victory bells rang out in German lands, and a boundless jubilation went throughout the whole of Germany. Belgium was overrun. Bold cavalrymen were already striking the gates of Paris. Would he be too late?

Finally, the big day arrived. His train went westward, but not at the furious speed of the express trains; the journey was slow:

> "At long last, the day came when we left Munich to fulfill our duty. For the first time in my life, I saw the Rhine; we journeyed westwards to stand guard before that historic German river, against its traditional and greedy enemy. As the first soft rays of the morning sun broke through the light mist, showing the Niederwald Statue, the whole transport train broke into strains of *Die Wacht am Rhein*. I felt as though my heart would burst."

Across the German border, past shattered houses and lonely villages, through the staging area, to the front. Then came a nocturnal march. Soon, bursts of shrapnel, and the troops found themselves under artillery fire, as the shells cracked and dirt splattered high into the air. The companies broke up into firing lines. Machine guns spewed death and destruction.

After four days of fierce fighting, man against man, the List Regiment turned back again. Thousands and thousands more spilled their blood with the song *Deutschland, Deutschland über alles* ('Germany, Germany Above All') on their lips. Hitler and his comrades had received their baptism of fire.

Days, weeks, months, and finally years passed. Every meter of ground was fought for with the severest hostility. France's soil was insatiable for German blood. Gone was the jubilation and enthusiasm of the August days. Calmness, determination, and deadly seriousness returned. The war volunteer became the tenacious, fearless, unbreakable and unyielding front soldier. He quietly did his duty. Hitler was appointed as a dispatcher and thus entrusted with the most dangerous task in the field. In the devastating barrage of fire, over craters, over the dead and the wounded, he had to establish contact with the troops fighting in others trenches; he had to deliver reports, no matter what: crawling or leaping, day and night, rain or shine.

Christmas was coming, and everyone wanted to be at home on Christmas Eve, if only for an hour. Hitler's comrades talked about it and looked forward to their mail packages from home. One of his comrades recalled, "Hitler stood aside and paid no attention to our conversation. He had little time for such requests. He had no interest in incoming mail parcels."

Wounded in the Battle of the Somme

When his comrades then fetched their packages and offered Hitler some of their delicacies, he always politely declined. He ate his plain rolls with jam and drank a canteen of tea.

They often wrangled over politics, and Hitler took a sharp stance against unreasonableness and bullying in the field. One member of the List Regiment tells of a telephone operator who, before the great autumn battle, said to him that he didn't give a damn whether Germany won or lost the war. Hitler got so angry that, if they hadn't stopped him, the operator would have been sent to the hospital with a bloody head.

For almost two years Hitler was always in the line of fire; he was never in the hospital, and he never went on vacation. "Since October 1914, he was always on the alert, never again sleeping in a bed." When he fell ill in December 1915, despite all attempts to persuade him, he did not report to the doctor but went about his work regardless of his ailing condition. He was later wounded in the Battle of the Somme on 7 October 1916. Only partially healed, he was soon again with his Regiment at the front.

For Conspicuous Valor

The German line withdrew. The List Regiment was on standby. In front of their position was a farmhouse where some German soldiers had taken shelter. The regimental commander told Adolf Hitler: "Take another man with you, and go forth to save our comrades from capture by the French!"

Cautiously, skillfully dodging enemy fire, the two went forward to meet the advancing enemy. No sooner had they reached the first house, when they actually heard the murmur of voices from the cellar of a bullet-riddled house. Acting quickly, Hitler jumped down the stairs to inform his comrades that the front was moving back. He threw open the door. There, what a shock! The cellar was full of Frenchmen! Hitler quickly grasped the situation, and shouted these words, in French, into the cellar: "Hands up! Weapons down! You are trapped! Leave the cellar in single file!" The dumbfounded French, daunted by the flashing barrel of the revolver, obeyed the command. They climbed the stairs and lined up to march off as prisoners.

Imagine how ashamed the French officer and his men were, when they realized that they had been taken prisoner by only two German soldiers! But imagine how happy Hitler and the whole regiment were, too, that this brave stunt had succeeded.

In recognition of his proven courage and his quick decision-making, Adolf Hitler received the Iron Cross 1st Class from the regimental commander.

2 — Munich

The War-Blinded

Even as Germany's sons bled to death on the battlefield, back home, inside the country, a cold and methodical spirit was growing, which had a terrible effect. There, cowards who opposed the war had only one concern: to save themselves, to undermine the sense of duty, and to destroy the will and determination to tenaciously persevere. Thus, from the homeland, attrition and decay came to the front. From out of the homeland, the stab in the back was perpetrated against the battling army. At the front itself, the air was purer and healthier than inside the country. Back home, Marxist criminals organized munitions strikes. The enemy's will to fight was revived, and in the face of enemy attacks, many German fighters died shortly before the end of the war.

At Ypres in October 1918, deadly mustard gas was discharged by the British. Gas grenades burst by the thousands. The ranks of fighters thinned out. One by one, they staggered back, screaming into the night from the pain in their burning eyes. Many fell down and lay there. Even Hitler faltered. He felt burning pain and tore at his eyes. Darkness surrounded him. He staggered back; then strong arms seized him and led him to the first-aid station. He opened his eyes as wide as he could, but saw only the blackness of night.

Hitler lay blinded in the Pasewalk hospital, in the far east of Germany. There he learned about the mutiny by the Navy. In the hospital courtyard, sailors went around with red ribbons and flags. The "revolution" had erupted. Great speeches were made, and the people were promised an empire of beauty, freedom, and dignity. Princes and kings were driven out of Germany, and Marxist Red worker- and soldier-councils seized control.

In utter despair, Hitler threw himself on his bed and wept over the shame and disgrace that had befallen the German people. A few days later, when the heavens restored his eyesight, he decided to become a politician.

The Politician

Hitler left the hospital and went to Munich in November 1918. He then moved to Traunstein with his old regiment. In the spring of 1919, he returned to Munich once again. The Jew Kurt Eisner had been shot by another Jew, Arco-Valley, and pure Moscow-style Bolsheviks terrorized the population. Hostages in the Luitpold gymnasium were murdered. They wanted to arrest Hitler, but the brutalized journeymen escaped from the loaded Red pistol. In fierce street fights from inside and out, Munich was eventually freed from the murderous rabble.

Hitler then became a training officer in the rifle regiment and thus had the opportunity to speak to soldiers every day. He was ordered to supervise a meeting of the *Deutsche Arbeiterpartei* (DAP, or 'German Workers' Party'). A conference took place in the Leiber room of the Sternecker Brewery. About 20 people were there, all common men.

Hitler spoke in the discussion. Then, a few days later, he received a postcard with the following message: "Dear Sir! The *German Workers' Party* has decided to accept you as its member. We kindly ask you to come to a committee meeting on Wednesday at the Alte Rosenbad Inn on Herrenstrasse and to comment on our above resolution." Hitler went to the meeting. First the minutes were read. The financial assessment showed just seven and a half marks in the bank.

Then various letters were read out and their responses determined. It was the worst kind of association imaginable. And yet Hitler made up his mind to join. He became member #7.

They met once a week in a small coffee house. The masses would have to be won over with extensive propaganda, Hitler declared, and so they prepared hundreds of invitations to the next meeting. Hitler himself delivered eighty of these. And the result? The same seven members were present.

But his courage did not falter. Additional meetings were scheduled. Three, thirteen, seventeen, then 34 listeners showed up. An advertisement for a new meeting was placed in a Munich newspaper. One hundred and eleven people came to the small meeting hall of the Hofbräuhaus. Hitler spoke, and at the end, he appealed to their willingness to make sacrifices. Several minutes of applause broke out and 300 marks in donations lay before the amazed treasurer. One gathering followed the other. The number of attendees climbed to 270.

Then, bright red posters called for the first large mass meeting in the Bürgerbräu. Two thousand people answered the call. Half the hall was filled with enemies: communists and social democrats. They wanted to break up the meeting. But groups of Hitler's comrades, in between students and young men, were spread around the room. Then

Hitler spoke and announced for the first time the Party's 25 Point Program. At that moment, roaring, jeering, and whistling began; there was a scuffle, chairs were thrown, and then after a great fight, it was quiet again. Hitler continued to speak and when he ended, applause erupted from the room.

Hitler then called the people to the Circus Krone. Six thousand came, later 8,000. Five large mass gatherings followed, totaling 14,000 people. Hitler responded to these five initial meetings with ten meetings in the largest halls in Munich, involving 20,000 people. Then colored Frenchmen marched into German territory and occupied the Ruhr area. Eighty thousand people protested with Hitler on the Königplatz.

Germany was at the end of its strength, and terrible inflation brought financial misery and despair. The autumn of 1923 was to be decisive for the future of Germany and for the Party.

November 9, 1923

The dissatisfaction of the German people with the government of the Weimar Republic grew steadily. They called for a man who would put an end to the misery and humiliation. Hitler was prepared to do this. There was a risk of open conflict between Bavaria and the German Reich. There was already talk of a march to Berlin. In the Bürgerbräukeller, Hitler proclaimed a national revolution and announced the new Reich government: Hitler, Ludendorff, and Pöhner. Ritter von Kahr, the State Commissioner of Bavaria, also agreed. But treachery was already was at work. In front of the Munich Feldherrnhalle, the first 12 martyrs of the movement fell dead to the banner of the reactionary forces. The national uprising collapsed. Hitler was arrested and sent to prison.

Hitler in Landsberg

Hitler was accused of high treason and sentenced to five years imprisonment. He sat in Landsberg prison for a year and a half. There he created his great work, *Mein Kampf*—the bible of the movement. The prisoners' cells were arranged around a common room. They were allowed outside their cells for just two hours a day; they were not subject to aggressive treatment, but they were deprived of their freedom.

While Hitler was inside his cell working on his book, outside, his movement was breaking up in a quarrel of opinions; the Führer—the Leader—was simply missing. Even when his signature was misused, he shut himself off completely and did not answer any more letters. Meanwhile, the disintegration of his movement continued. On a walk with his assistant Rudolf Hess, he spoke these words: "I tell you, after this collapse, it will take five years before I can rebuild the party!"

And he was right.

Confinement in Prison

Chapter 3
The Struggle for Power

Germany awaken!

1. The Organizer

In the year 1925, Adolf Hitler began his great struggle for the liberation of Germany. As he left Landsberg Fortress, the gates closed behind him. Drum beats of promotion pounded tirelessly to shake up all fellow Germans, even those with their caps pulled down over their eyes. Calls of "Germany, awaken!" resounded in the streets of the big cities and on the country roads all over Germany. The newspaper *Völkischer Beobachter* ("People's Observer"), which had been banned for a long time, was permitted to reappear, announcing the spirit of Hitler in all German districts and professing the ideas of National Socialism to the whole world. Our Fatherland must become free again.

A large mass meeting convened in Munich, with Adolf Hitler as the speaker. The crowd was tremendous. Many thousands wanted to hear the words of the leader who had been imprisoned for so long. In his speech, he implored all those who shared his goals to stand together again in unison and to trust and agree to his leadership. That day signified the reestablishment of the National Socialist movement; it became the second great starting point in the struggle for German freedom.

However, this rally, which was inspiring for everyone, was also to be the prelude to the constant and extreme persecutions that were carried out in the years that followed. The report on Adolf Hitler's speech, falsely described by hostile newspaper reporters, prompted the Bavarian government to impose a long-term ban on Hitler speaking in public. All the governments of the German states, whether they were governed by Marxism or by the center, took part in the harshest persecution of the NSDAP since 1925. Although the Imperial Constitution, created in this political system, solemnly guaranteed the rights of freedom and justice for every citizen, they were nevertheless handled in an entirely biased and one-sided manner. In the eyes of the government, every National Socialist was a second-class citizen.

Adolf Hitler was illegally prevented from promoting his ideas. The coming years were marked by the rebuilding of the organization. The principle governing this activity was based upon the idea that the NSDAP is not only a political party, but above all it is a movement that demands the complete reorganization of German life. Various sub-organizations are created that carry the National Socialist spirit into the individual ethnic groups and social classes. The National Socialist German Student Association was formed, which prepared German students for life in the National Socialist state. The Hitler Youth was brought into being, precisely in order to prepare German boys and girls for the task that they would later have to fulfill. All German youth are destined to take up Hitler's legacy one day, so they must be trained so that they can administer it correctly and effectively. German boys and girls love and revere the Führer, because he will make their lives better and secure their future. The old politicians of appeasement made our youth into slaves of hostile foreign countries; Hitler gave the German youth their freedom.

The National Socialist Association of Legal Professionals and the National Socialist League of German Doctors examined the legal and biological prerequisites that are necessary for the mental and physical liberation of our people. Hans Schemm devised a plan for a very large community of German educators in which all German teachers and instructors, Kindergarten teachers, handicraft teachers, elementary, middle, and university teachers, and pastors are brought together with a unified will and a single mission. In 1927, Schemm founded the National Socialist Teachers' League in the town of Hof, which sought to imbue all teachers with the spirit that is necessary for the education of the German youth as defined by Adolf Hitler.

This is how the NSDAP quietly took shape during these years. The organization made its appearance at the powerful party conferences in Weimar in 1926 and in Nuremberg in 1927 and 1929, and provided cohesion and oversight for the large number of members throughout Germany.

2. Further Attempts at Suppression

With joyful satisfaction, Adolf Hitler, the supreme leader of the *Sturmabteilung* (SA), followed the powerful development of his "Brownshirted Army." The loyal, self-sacrificing fighters marched at all rallies and meetings to show the enemies of the party that the National Socialist movement had great power behind it. The enemies could only attack by cowardly ambushes. Day after day, SA men, with their unwavering enthusiasm and willingness to fight for the ideas of National Socialism, paid with their lives to fortify their Fatherland. They, too, died a hero's death on the field of honor. But despite these aggressions, and perhaps precisely because of these attacks, the *Sturmabteilung* ('Storm Battalion') grew at an incredible rate. Every SA man considered it his most sacred task and duty to his Führer to use all his strength, indeed his life, for the liberation of our people from the Black and Red forces.

Comrades shot by the Red Front

Then, an unparalleled wave of persecution set in. The government prohibited the National Socialists from wearing their uniforms. The brown-shirted SA men had their shirts pulled off in the streets. Their meetings were monitored. Every word of the speakers was written down. Any criticism of Red dignitaries and the leaders of the center parties was met with severe penalties. Hundreds of National Socialist speakers and writers were banned—not for a few days, but for many months. The legal system did not help them. Every SA protest was dismissed with a sneer. Civil servants who supported National Socialism were harassed or hounded from their posts.

If you don't risk your life, you will never win it.

The People awaken. Young Germany is marching.

The Catholic Church even issued decrees proclaiming that National Socialists could no longer receive either a church burial or the holy sacraments. The National Socialists, who led the bitter fight against the atheist movement, who wanted to destroy the godless Communists, who protected the Church and fought for its rights, were lumped together with the Bolsheviks. It was an attack on the honor and truthfulness of the National Socialist movement—but they totally misjudged Hitler's sincere intentions.

The goal of all these governmental persecutions was the annihilation and destruction of this original German movement. But the healthy forces of National Socialism, set deep within the people, were stronger than their opponents. Every individual was compelled by these persecutions to grapple even more intimately with the ideas of Adolf Hitler. The more people engaged with the movement's ideas, the more enthusiastic and steadfast they became as followers. The persecutions became a purifying fire; the idea of National Socialism, and the liberation of the German people, took hold more and more.

3. Towards the Goal

Adolf Hitler was an enemy of parliamentarism. Many parties sat in the German government, the Reichstag—and they all disagreed. According to an old saying, "When seven Germans get together, there are eight opinions." The parties no longer thought of the welfare of their great German Fatherland, but only of their own small party interests. That is why Hitler rejected the party state. The NSDAP was not supposed to be a "party," but rather *a movement* that encompassed the entire German people. Hitler wanted to create his own German people that would not tear itself apart through internal discord.

But nevertheless, the National Socialists, though they were opponents of parliament, had no choice except to work through the Reichstag. Hitler did not want to become Reich leader by force, but rather, legally and constitutionally. At first, only a small group of 12 NSDAP representatives won elections. The other parties mocked them, but they stood firm. They kept walking their straight path without looking left or right; and they said: "Someday, you will all join us!"

Then, in the autumn of 1930, a mighty National Socialist storm rose up and swept over the German people. On 14 September 1930, the day of the Reichstag election, the number of National Socialist deputies rose from 12 to 107. A glorious victory was achieved. The whole world listened; the whole world recognized that Adolf Hitler could no longer be ignored. The future then belonged to National Socialism.

Now, there was no holding back. People no longer sat quietly with their hands in their lap. Each victory gave the fighters an obligation to do even more. Hitler never rested. He was not satisfied with one million followers; he wanted ten million, he wanted 60 million, he wanted the whole people. His call was: "It must be all of Germany!"

4. The Speaker

The people's hardship continued to grow; the army of unemployed rose monstrously, and the government was increasingly helpless in the face of circumstances. Incompetence was the hallmark of the Red and Black rulers.

Despite a huge burden, his heart beats for every Hitler youth

It is a great time: all eyes are on Adolf Hitler, the savior from all troubles. His followers increase day by day.

In two rounds of voting on March 13 and April 10, 1932, Hitler ran against Paul von Hindenburg. Hitler collected 14 million votes, but since the Marxists and the Center Party voted for Hindenburg—only to stop Hitler—Hindenburg emerged victorious with 19 million votes.

Finally, the Center Party Chancellor, Heinrich Brüning, who bent over backwards to persecute the National Socialists, fell from power. At this point, there was great relief among the German people, but still, the government did not decide to appoint Hitler as Chancellor. Instead, Franz von Papen became Chancellor, and he allowed the National Socialists to campaign freely across the country. Then the Führer Hitler raced through the whole of Germany, by airplane and by car. He held five or six enormous rallies every day, in every major city of the Reich. Everywhere he found the same level of glorious enthusiasm.

The largest and most spacious halls were not large enough to accommodate the vast crowds who wanted to hear the Führer. Long before the start of his speech, the hall must be closed by the police. All the other halls in the city, where the speech is broadcast through loud speakers, fill up. One by one, they are closed due to overcrowding. In front of the hall, the crowds are waiting for Adolf Hitler, in order to see the star of hope for the German people, or to hear the speech broadcast in the open air. The German people are enthusiastic and excited whenever Hitler speaks. Everyone comes to hear him. Next to the worker sits the professor, next to the pastor the farmer, next to the craftsman the teacher, and next to the unemployed the entrepreneur. And they all feel connected by the unifying bond of Germany, to which all our love is directed.

Euphoric enthusiasm, a sea of raised hands, and prolonged shouts of praise welcome the Führer. He stands on the grandstand in front of the microphone, which carries the sound of his voice to the others awaiting eagerly.

"... you must learn to respect yourselves again."

A movement of his hand creates the necessary calm. All eyes are fixed on him. He stands tall and straight in front of the crowd. His serious, sensitive, expressive eyes roam over the multitude. In a deep, sonorous voice, calm, clear and deliberate, he begins his remarks.

Everyone listens intently to his introductory words. One could hear a pin drop. A quarter- or even a half-an-hour goes by without applause breaking out. Hitler forces his listeners to follow his train of thought. He prepares everyone, and directs their attitude and way of thinking to the path he is following. He has no need for any pieces of paper on which he has jotted down critical points. The thoughts that he strings together flow logically from deep within him. Each sentence is a model of the German flair for language. Each paragraph is a self-contained thought. Every speech is a perfection, a complete totality. Nothing is forgotten, everything is said that must be said in order to tear the bandages from people's eyes, in order to open their eyes to the plight of the people and the incompetence of their rulers, to kindle an enthusiastic commitment to National Socialism. Storms of enthusiasm roar through the room when he ruthlessly settles the score with the enemies of the German people. His deepest devotion to his German people, for whose liberation he spared no sacrifice, is met with the most joyful approval.

Whoever hears Hitler is under his spell, and is electrified by him. Every speech brings many new registrations to the NSDAP. Every speech is accompanied by unprecedented success. Adolf Hitler achieves victory wherever he uses his power. Is it any wonder that the Marxists and the Center Party, who ruled in Germany, failed to bring his triumphal march to a halt? Their complete defeat and destruction are linked to his victory.

On 31 July 1932, the Reichstag parliamentary elections earned the NSDAP the tremendous number of 230 deputies. However, the time was not yet ripe. What used to be the usual practice, that the leader of the strongest faction was charged with forming the government, is no longer observed. Our leader was offered the post of Vice Chancellor, which he naturally declined. The German people demand a fundamental change of politics in the spirit of the National Socialist worldview.

5. The Imperial Chancellor

After a short interlude, Hitler was finally named as Reich Chancellor by General von Schleicher; thus, the longing of most of the people was fulfilled. In the midday hours of 30 January 1933, which became a momentous day, news of the earth-shattering event raced thorough out the world: Hitler had been appointed Reich Chancellor.

Hitler's appointment as the leader of German destiny was not only welcomed by a few insiders. Tears of joy and gratitude also welled up in the eyes of millions of Germans upon hearing the news.

Even when the events of the time, the struggle for the monumental growth of National Socialist freedom movement, finally achieved their goal, it was still an extraordinary and astonishing surprise. Years had gone by, and two decades of German suffering were in the past. The poverty was terrible. The struggle was ruthless and often brutal. Hundreds of the best Germans paid with their lives in the Great War for the goal of freedom. Hundreds of thousands of good Germans sank with this last hope into their graves.

It was achieved! Hitler flags were indeed fluttering over every street. The rejoicing of 12 million of the best and most committed National Socialist fighters knew no bounds. In the lives of contemporaries, this moment, when the National Socialism seized power, can only be compared to the experience of start of the Great War on 2 August 1914, when nameless men and women shook hands in the street and swore allegiance—for the greatness and power of Germany.

SA and steel helmet troops gathered in Berlin to pay homage to the venerable Reich President and the young Reich Chancellor through an endless torchlight procession. The marching columns echoed through the peace and quiet of a Berlin evening into the late hours of the night. Hindenburg waited at the window of the Presidential palace until the last group has passed. At the window of the Reich Chancellery, Adolf Hitler greeted his brave SA comrades and the steel-helmet brigades with his right hand raised.

Hitler immediately dissolved the Reichstag in order to give all the people the opportunity to accept or reject his new government. The decision was made on March 5th. Finally, no more election propaganda. The struggle ended in success. A majority of the German people professed their support for Hitler and his government. The national revolution was complete. The people overcame the disgrace of 1918—this un-German revolt—and found their way back to themselves. What had tragically failed again and again, finally become a reality.

6. The Day of Potsdam

No one who traveled the path between Berlin and Potsdam will ever forget it. Only when you look at the two-thousand-year history of German people together, do you realize the greatness of what had transpired. One feels especially proud of the harmony of the great goals of Richard Wagner and Houston Stewart Chamberlain with the great political events of those days in Potsdam. The connection, the unifying idea that stretched from Potsdam via Weimar to Bayreuth, was clearly visible. These three locations restored themselves, and the opera *Meistersinger*, which was more performed in the Berlin State Opera, once again makes clear the unity and connectedness of these three.

The scene at Potsdam: cathedral; Garrison Church; organ tones; gathering together; Brahms; choir singing…all these things heralded the moral force of a new age, in contrast to the blasphemy of 1918. Reich President von Hindenburg appeared in a general's uniform, while Chancellor Adolf Hitler and the Reich government entered the church of the Prussian kings.

Then the Reich President spoke to the breathless silence of the assembled representatives of the people, representatives of foreign powers, and ministers. He then turned over the floor to our Reich Chancellor Adolf Hitler. The Führer interpreted the meaning of the day in an incomparable way.

Thus, the political-racial, religious, sacred act found its ultimate completion. Standing, those present listened to the final words of the leader. It was as if the crypt of a great king opened and he was walking through the rows of those assembled. He said: "At last, you have found me again. Now, as then, you are going upward and forward!" The whole emotion and the seriousness of the hour was on everyone's faces. The sounds of the organ penetrated quietly into the heart, while von Hindenburg lay down the laurel wreath at the tomb of Frederick the Great.

At this very moment, the dark clouds vanished from the sky. Glorious blueness shone down. When people first entered the church, the sky was grey. But the dark clouds over the church passed away. This occurrence was also symbolic of the meaning this act of state had for the German people. When Hitler finished, beams of sunlight broke through the church windows. It was as if the Lord God wanted to hail the new Germany with his sun, which prayed for strength and blessings for the new work of creation.

Then the church emptied, and outside—glittering sunshine. At the end of this long ceremony, dazzling spring sun. Marching army battalions, swelling drum rolls, the band began to play, the old army arose. Then, the shouts of "Heil!" and the never-ending cheers from hundreds of thousands. Untold masses of people in Potsdam had a stupendous, joyous, inner experience.

May the old spirit of this place of glory continue to inspire today's generation, may it free us from selfishness and sectarian strife, and bring us together in national self-reflection and spiritual renewal for the blessing of a united, free, proud Germany!

Heil Hitler!

3 — The Struggle for Power

⦅⦆⦅⦆⦅⦆⦅⦆⦅⦆⦅⦆⦅⦆⦅⦆⦅⦆⦅⦆⦅⦆

A personal note from Hitler:

You, German youth, are the coming people, and the completion of what we are fighting for today rests on you. Just as you, my German boys and girls, are already striving for the well-being of our people in your common struggle, so too are millions of adult men and women fighting for Germany's resurgence. National Socialism created a national community that begins with children and ends with the elderly. You too, my German boys and girls, should strive for the German community in the future, beyond everything that divides you, and happily serve it with your whole being. Never forget: one day, you will be Germany.

Adolf Hitler

His life, his struggles, his striving is for your future, German youth!

For Further Reading:

Hitler, A. 2022. *Mein Kampf*, 2 volumes (T. Dalton, trans.). Clemens & Blair.

The classic work by Hitler, this lengthy book is partly autobiography, partly political manifesto, and partly philosophical worldview. In it, Hitler tackles a variety of controversial topics including race, religion, critiques of democracy, and what to do about the Jewish Question.

Hitler, A. 2019. *The Essential Mein Kampf* (T. Dalton, trans.). Clemens & Blair.

This is a condensed, one-volume version of *Mein Kampf*. It contains all the most interesting and most relevant passages, and leaves out much material that is only of marginal interest today. This is the best choice for first-time readers of *Mein Kampf*.

Hiemer, E. 2020. *The Poisonous Mushroom*. Clemens & Blair.

A collection of 17 short stories intended for young children ages 8 to 14, addressing specifically the Jewish Question: namely, what children should watch out for, and how they can avoid being harmed by Jews. Originally published in German in 1938 with the title *Der Giftpilz*, this book contains 18 drawings by the famous artist Fips.

Dalton, T. 2019. *The Jewish Hand in the World Wars*. Clemens & Blair.

Much has been written on World Wars One and Two, but almost nothing has been said about the important role that Jews played in starting both wars. Here, Dr. Dalton gives the basic facts and identifies specific Jews in Europe and the US, and he demonstrates that they were central to both wars.

Dalton, T. 2020. *Eternal Strangers: Critical Views of Jews and Judaism through the Ages*. Clemens & Blair.

For well over 2,000 years, Jews have displayed an arrogance and even a hatred of other people—of all who were not Jews. This, in turn, caused other people to hate them. In this book, Dr. Dalton compiles a list of critical comments of Jews by dozens of famous thinkers and writers throughout history. He demonstrates that so-called 'anti-Semitism' is both rational and justified.

Penman, R. 2021. *Pan-Judah! Political Cartoons of Der Stürmer* (2 volumes). Clemens & Blair.

The artist Fips, who created all the drawings in *German Youth*, also created hundreds of cartoons of Jews for the newspaper *Der Stürmer*, between 1925 and 1945. In these two books, Robert Penman has restored and colorized 200 cartoons in each. The images are vivid, sharp, humorous, and enlightening.

APPENDIX

The following are a few images from the original 1934 German book, *Deutsche Jugend, Dein Fuhrer!*

Braunau liegt unmittelbar an der bayerisch-österreichischen Grenze, die durch den Inn gebildet ist. Dort wurde Adolf Hitler als Sohn des Zollbeamten Alois Hitler und seiner Gattin Klara geboren. Nicht lange nach seiner Geburt wurde der Vater nach Passau versetzt. Um seiner Familie ein ständiges Heim zu bieten, kaufte er in dem nahe gelegenen Dorf Hafeld an der Traun ein ländliches Besitztum, welches nun für längere Zeit der ständige Wohnsitz der Familie war. Er selbst konnte nur an Sonn- und Feiertagen dorthin zurückkehren, da es sein anstrengender Dienst nicht erlaubte. Später nahm er den Abschied und wurde wieder Bauer, wie es einst seine Väter waren. Es waren glückliche Jahre, die der junge Knabe im ländlichen Hause der Eltern, in der mit Getreidefeldern, Wiesen und Gärten gesegneten Landschaft verleben durfte. Was ein Knabenherz nur begehren kann, war ihm geboten: zum Klettern die zum Himmel ragenden Birken und Erlen, zum Springen die Bach, der dicht am väterlichen Garten vorbeifloß. Auch die Arbeit im landwirtschaftlichen Betrieb machte dem Jungen große Freude. Besondere Zuneigung hatte er zu den jungen Tieren des Hofes, mit denen er herumtollte und spielte, als wären sie seine besten Kameraden. Seine liebsten Spielgefährten waren ihm die Hunde, deren treue Anhänglichkeit er auch heute noch hoch schätzt.

Der Tierfreund.

Vater und Mutter.

— 5 —

Der junge Revolutionär.

"Ich war alles andere als ein braver Junge im landläufigen Sinne, — ich war ein kleiner Rädelsführer geworden." Hitler.

Der Führer erzählt von sich selbst, daß er in der Schule leicht und sehr gut lernte, „sonst aber ziemlich schwierig zu behandeln war". Seine prächtige Auffassungsgabe, sein reiches Innenleben, das besonders gekennzeichnet ist durch plötzlich auftretende, blitzartig einsehende Eingebungen ermöglichten es ihm wohl sehr leicht und gründlich, mit dem im Unterricht zur Behandlung stehenden Stoff fertig zu werden. Sein klarer Geist erkannte sehr bald Wesentliches vom Unwesentlichen zu unterscheiden und somit ein festgefügtes, bestgeordnetes Wissen anzueignen. Dem begabten Schüler stand dann außerdem noch genügend Zeit zur Verfügung, um neben der Betätigung im Haushalt auch dem Herumtummeln im Freien mit den Altersgenossen sich hinzugeben. Der Wohnort der Eltern bot ihm hierzu reichliche Veranlassung. Hitler hatte das hohe Glück, seine Jugendjahre auf dem Lande, in Feld, Wiese und Wald zubringen zu dürfen. Da konnte sich denn der Mut und die Entschlossenheit des Knaben, die Unternehmungslust und die Freude an der frischfrohen Tat schon bald entwickeln. Es war ihm eine besondere Lust schon als Knabe, bestehende Schwierigkeiten zu überwinden und den Kampf auch mit Altersgenossen jederzeit gerne und

ritterlich aufzunehmen. Beulen und Wunden wurden dabei willig mit hingenommen. Unerträglich aber war ihm der Gedanke, irgend etwas im Leben nicht erreichen zu können. Hatte er in einer Auseinandersetzung mit den oft recht robusten Jugendgenossen einen Schmerz oder eine Wunde erlitten, so verabscheute er es, Hilfe etwa auch bei der sorgenden Mutter zu suchen. Die Selbständigkeit und das mutige Ertragen von Unannehmlichkeiten des Lebens waren dem Knaben schon in den frühesten Jugendjahren sehr zu eigen.

Nichts verabscheute er so sehr als die Verweichlichung, die Stubenhockerei. So wie sich beim Erwachsenen der Charakter nur „im Strome der Welt" bilden kann, so kann erst recht beim Kinde nur der Umgang mit Altersgenossen die Voraussetzung bilden für den späteren Lebenskampf.

Schon sehr frühzeitig lernte er daher auch, sich mit den Schattenseiten des Menschen auseinanderzusetzen. Ungezogenheiten seiner Kameraden, begangene Fehler, die bestimmt eine Strafe nach sich gezogen hätten, wußte er mit Schweigsamkeit zu ertragen. Dem jugendlichen Freunde freilich redete er ins Gewissen. Mit aller Eindringlichkeit wußte er dessen Unrecht nachzuweisen. Wiederholte er aber die Untat und hatten Warnungen und freundschaftliche Mahnungen nichts, so konnte er auch unerbittlich sein und die Freundschaft für eine Zeitlang oder auch für immer auflagen.

Dem begabten Jungen, dessen starke charakterliche Prägung den Kameraden sehr bald bemerkt wurde, fehlte es natürlich auch nicht an Feindschaften von seiten der Altersgenossen. Sehr häufig stand der junge Adolf in Streitfällen allein und eine heute Schmeicher stand Lust und Willen, sich mit den Stärkeren auseinanderzusetzen.

Ein Mitschüler Hitlers schreibt über eine derartige Begebenheit: Eines Tages gab eine Rotte Buben die Losung aus, heute nachmittag nach der Schule „walsch'n mit'n Hitler". Auf zum Kampf Hitler ahnte selbstverständlich nichts von dem geplanten Überfall. Als er nun merkte, was geschehen sollte, wich er der Übermacht nicht aus, wie es andere in solchen Fällen getan hätten, sondern er nahm den Kampf an, obwohl er wenig Aussicht auf Erfolg hatte. Das „Walsh'n" ging aber nicht so tapfer, es ging Aug' um Aug', Zahn um Zahn. Um Bewegungsfreiheit zu haben und nicht unter Umklammerung zum Opfer zu fallen, löste er sich zu der Übermacht

— 15 —

www.ingramcontent.com/pod-product-compliance
Lightning Source LLC
LaVergne TN
LVHW061625070526
838199LV00070B/6588